The *First* Speaking and Listening Kit

Helen F. Hadley

Stanley Thornes (Publishers) Ltd

Contents

Teacher's Notes

Introduction	1
Key Elements in the Pupils' Sheets	1
The Four Elements	2
Speaking, Listening and Thinking	4
Speaking and Listening in the Classroom	6
Getting Children to Listen	8
Drama	9
Group Work	9
Assessment	10
Using the Sheets	10
Notes on the Use of Each Sheet	11

Activity Sheets

Who Lives Here?	20
Asim Wants a Biscuit	21
Where is My Home?	22
Who are You?	23
What's the Message?	24
What am I?	25
Sorting and Setting 1	26
Story Board	27
Wishing	28
Choices	29
Question and Answer	30
My Giant Sandwich	31
I Didn't Mean To . . .	32
Caged	33
Word Wall Puzzle	34
Party Time	35
The Wind and the Sun	36
My Home	37
Favourite Things	38
Goldilocks and the Three Bears	39
Finding Out	40
Mystery Parcel	41
Spot the Changes	42
What am I Looking At?	43
Guess What!	44
Telephone Talk 1	45
Poems We Like	46
Toy Shop	47
Our Senses	48
Our Senses – Likes and Dislikes	49
Calamity Kitchen	50
Choosing Colours	51
Colours – Warm or Cool	52
Colours for Reasons	53
Sorting and Setting 2	54
Birthday Wheel	55
Work	56
Sound Words	57
Telephone Talk 2	58
What's it all About?	59
Owning Up	60
What do you Know?	61

Teacher's Assessment Sheet 62

Text © Helen F. Hadley 1992
Original line illustrations by Andrew Keylock © ST(P) Ltd 1992

The right of Helen Hadley to be identified as author of this work has been asserted by her in accordance with the Copyright, Designs and Patents Act 1988.

The copyright holders authorise ONLY users of the *First Speaking and Listening Kit* to make photocopies or stencil duplicates of the pupils' sheets for their own or their classes' immediate use within the teaching context.

No other rights are granted without permission in writing from the publisher or under licence from the Copyright Licensing Agency Limited. Further details of such licences (for reprographic reproduction) may be obtained from the Copyright Licensing Agency Limited, of 90 Tottenham Court Road, London W1P 9HE.

Copying by any other means or for any other purpose is strictly prohibited without the prior written consent of the copyright holders.

Applications for such permission should be addressed to the publishers: Stanley Thornes (Publishers) Ltd, Old Station Drive, Leckhampton, CHELTENHAM GL53 0DN, England.

First published in 1992 by:
Stanley Thornes (Publishers) Ltd
Old Station Drive
Leckhampton
CHELTENHAM GL53 0DN
England

A catalogue record for this book is available from the British Library.

ISBN 0 7487 1488 X

Typeset by Tech-Set, Gateshead
Printed and bound in Great Britain by Ebenezer Baylis, Worcester

Cover photograph: ZEFA photo library.

Teacher's Notes

Introduction

The *Speaking and Listening Kit* is based upon the National Curriculum Programmes of Study and consists of two books, one for Key Stage 1 and another for Key Stage 2. Each book, has two parts: teacher's notes and copymasters or activity sheets. The teacher's notes introduce the material and suggest ways of working with it. A grid shows at a glance the titles of the activity sheets, the main areas they cover and their level of difficulty.

Speaking and Listening Activities

English from 5 to 16 calls for a substantial increase in the attention given to the spoken word saying that it should be employed for 'real or realistic purposes' wherever possible, in conjunction with written language modes. It also reminds us that spoken language teaching should cover issues of presentation, response to argument, reasoning, using evidence, validating and the development of personal and social skills.

Speaking and listening has moved a long way from the seen but not heard attitudes of previous decades to the extent that it is expected to arise naturally out of given tasks. No one would deny the value of this natural growth, but if children are to become skilled masters of spoken language, then the development of speaking and listening must not be left to chance. They need to encounter situations which require them to use more elaborate forms of language through which they are motivated to extend their level of language complexity.

The Kit

The *First Speaking and Listening Kit* provides a variety of interesting material to encourage a wide range of spoken language skills to:
- promote active listening
- stimulate discussion
- seek information
- provide explanation
- increase vocabulary
- suggest ways of presenting acquired knowledge
- provide models which can be adapted for other subjects.

Activities are also intended to:
- improve and increase attention span
- increase auditory discrimination
- extend vocabulary.

Language games are included because they make useful and lively additions to the activities provided for children to work from.

The Speaking and Listening Activity Sheets

In the *First Speaking and Listening Kit* the activity sheets develop both structure and progression in spoken language during the early primary years.

Within most spoken language situations there are four components:

- the person who says something
- the person to whom it is said
- the subject spoken about
- the context in which it is placed.

Each of these is present in the activities.

The sheets provide work for the whole class, small groups or pairs:
- to explore ideas and concepts
- to develop discussion and collaboration skills
- to gain information or seek explanation
- as a basis for performance
- as preparation for writing
- for prediction
- to develop personal and social communication skills.

They are organised with progression in mind but teachers may wish to select tasks which develop a particular skill or concept or are suited to a particular pupil. Different frames of reference can be applied to the same sheet. They can also be used for more able pupils or for pupils needing further experience in a particular aspect to revisit and work from a different standpoint. Earlier tasks can be referred back to (as reinforcement) for a pair or small group who are having problems with a more difficult activity. Follow up activities suggest ways of exploring the results of their work through discussion, presentation, performance, art and some extension ideas.

The National Curriculum

At Key Stage 1 (AT1, Programmes of Study) stress is placed on the need for children to 'encounter a range of situations, audiences and activities which are designed to develop their competence, precision and confidence in speaking and listening, irrespective of their initial competence or home language'. Consequently, intervention to assist a child's development must build on what s/he brings to the classroom environment, not be limited by it.

The recommendations of the National Curriculum's Programmes of Study can be grouped into four main elements:
- discussion and collaboration
- information and explanation
- personal and social
- presentation and performance.

The activity sheets are grouped under these headings in the grid on page 2 but other aspects of spoken and written language also feature in the activities.

Key Elements in the Pupils' Sheets

Note: All the activities involve discussion and collaboration, which is the essence of talking together, but they have only been marked on the grid where they are the dominant elements.

Teacher's Notes

	Discuss and collaborate	Inform and explain	Personal and social	Present and perform
Who Lives Here?	1	1		
Asim Wants a Biscuit	1		1	
Where is my Home?	1	1		
Who are You?				1
What's the Message?			1	
What am I?	1	1		
Sorting and Setting 1		1		
Story Board	1			
Wishing	1			
Choices			1	1
Question and Answer	1	1		
My Giant Sandwich			1	1
I Didn't Mean To . . .	1		1	
Caged			1	
Word Wall Puzzle	2			
Party Time	2	2		
The Wind and the Sun			2	2
My Home		2	2	
Favourite Things	2	2		
Goldilocks and the Three Bears	2			2
Finding Out	2	2		
Mystery Parcel	2			2
Spot the Changes		2		
What am I Looking At?	2	2	2	
Guess What!		2		2
Telephone Talk 1			2	2
Poems We Like	2			2
Toy Shop	3	3		
Our Senses		3	3	
Our Senses – Likes and Dislikes		3		
Calamity Kitchen	3	3	3	3
Choosing Colours	3			3
Colours – Warm or Cool	3			3
Colour for Reasons		3		
Sorting and Setting 2		3		
Birthday Wheel		3	3	
Work				3
Sound Words		3	3	
Telephone Talk 2		3	3	3
What's it all About?			3	3
Owning Up	3		3	
What do you Know?	3	3		

The numbers indicate levels of difficulty.

The Four Elements

Like the four modes of language, the four main elements of speaking and listening are interwoven with each other, yet need to be identified separately in order that awareness is raised of their contribution to the whole. In the activity sheets this interweaving is evident but emphasis is laid on one element more than the others.

Discussion and Collaboration
The National Curriculum Programmes of Study state the need for children to be able to discuss their work with others, to talk about their experience in and out of school and work in collaboration with groups of varying sizes. The *First Speaking and Listening Kit* requires children to discuss the activities with each other and to collaborate in order to complete them.

The need to talk We all need to talk about the day-to-day things that happen to us and matter to us in our daily lives. We need to share our innermost thoughts and feelings. There must be time and freedom for this aspect of talk within school but if children's spoken language skills are to be extended beyond the day-to-day, structured provision must be made for this to take place.

Teacher's Notes

Focusing the talk   Talk needs to be focused if it is to be productive; it must require collaboration through pooling ideas and making decisions, e.g. problem-solving activities. If the task is practical, talk is practical, but if discussion is the main focus regarding an issue without the need for practical decisions then the talk produced seems to be more sustained and 'on task'. However, if the task can be achieved while talking about last night's activities or a TV programme, it will!

Engaging their interest   The subject must be one which engages the children's interest if you want discussion rather than chat, for example:
- shared experiences – story, topic, visit, visitors
- experiments or investigations
- making working models
- own toys and treasures
- pictures and photographs
- stuffed animals and other artefacts – museum loan
- appropriate topics to argue or debate (e.g. should children have to earn their pocket money? Should boys and girls be able to play with the same toys or do the same activities?).

Collaboration   Working together has to grow from the egocentricity of the nursery child to the fullness of debate during the primary years. Initially children work alongside each other so the first step is to learn to work in pairs before moving on to a group situation. The *First Speaking and Listening Kit* extends children's ability to collaborate effectively through a range of activities on varied topics in different groupings.

Language play   In order to be able to express themselves clearly in discussion, a good command of language and a wide vocabulary are needed. Having fun together by playing with words enables children to use language in a more relaxed way and to collaborate together while assisting the growth of their spoken language, for example through:
- I Spy, riddles, jokes, play on words, crosswords
- Twenty Questions, TV game shows
- tapes of instructions, treasure hunts, seek and find
- group poems and rhymes
- media words created to catch the public's attention.

Information and Explanation
If we listened to ourselves during the course of a day we would be surprised at the amount of information we imparted or extracted and the extent to which we explained our actions, our findings, or how we performed a task. The National Curriculum Programmes of Study point to the need for children to be able to give and receive simple explanations, information and instructions and to respond to visual and aural stimuli. The *First Speaking and Listening Kit* provides opportunities for children to develop their spoken language skills through activities which can be adapted to other areas of the curriculum.

Something to learn   By active listening children gain access to the ideas, knowledge and feelings of others. If the listening task has outcomes – information to be used, an ending to be predicted, a reason for a course of action to be explained, etc. – listening will be active not passive. Through spoken language, knowledge can be converted into understanding. For example, by listening to an explanation then conveying the concept to others we come to understand it better. Also, through working and talking with others we may come to a new understanding which we might not have reached on our own.

If children are sometimes given the opportunity to set the purpose and ask the questions, e.g. in research, topic work, problem-solving, they have a real need to pay attention because they are committed to the outcome.

Something worthwhile to achieve   Children need to feel that the activity or task they are involved in is worthwhile. This can come from the task itself or its outcome. Children can explain their work to others – teacher, peers (class or group) or parents – or present it by display or in a performance of some kind. Other activities could include devising rules that affect their community, taking messages, answering the telephone, showing visitors around the school or helping a peer or a younger child to understand a problem.

Dialogue with a more skilled person is a powerful means of learning for a child whether that person be a teacher, an enquiring adult or a pupil, because, by asking the right kind of questions, children can be directed along more productive paths than they might pursue on their own and so achieve a more satisfactory result.

Personal and Social
The National Curriculum Programmes of Study highlight the need for children to have a grasp of turn-taking, to be able to voice disagreement courteously, to give weight to the opinions of others, to articulate personal feelings and to adjust and adapt to views expressed. These skills, which have often been part of a school's 'hidden' curriculum, have been consciously built in to the *First Speaking and Listening Kit's* activities.

Internal   Being able to use spoken language competently, to speak easily and freely in front of others, to give voice to thoughts and ideas confidently, increases our self-concept and we develop the ability to present and discuss our views, opinions and thoughts to others without feeling rejected, as a person, if others disagree.

Interactive   Most language growth takes place through interaction. We interpret what others say in line with our knowledge and experience. To be able to take a leading part in debate, to perform in a way that holds an audience's attention (however large or small that may be), to present data and argue its conclusions are life skills which give us the confidence to stand up for what we believe and enable us to play a useful part in the community.

Social   Through spoken languages we learn social mores of greeting, thanking and small talk. We learn how to enquire or register complaint in an acceptable manner, to tease, tell anecdotes or the happenings in our lives, to express our feelings and to be verbally at ease in most situations. We also learn from personal contact, from story and from study about the lives and social mores of other cultures.

Teacher's Notes

Presentation and Performance

Some children are born performers, others shrink from it. Some children confidently display their skills and talents through a variety of forms of display and presentation (AT1 L4d), others do not know where to begin.

The first Statement of Attainment for speaking and listening is clear: 'pupils should be able to participate as speakers and listeners in group activities, including imaginative play'. The National Curriculum Programmes of Study also include the need for children to be involved in role-play, to listen and talk to audiences of different sizes and to take part in imaginative play and improvised drama. A number of suggestions for presentation and performance are in the *First Speaking and Listening Kit*.

Something to say   Children must be at ease with the subject they are to talk about and the words they have to say – whether they are to present a play, a poem, a character from a story, role-play, talk about a personal treasure, an experiment or act as the spokesperson for a group activity. They must know the content well and, if the occasion demands, have time to practise so that it is familiar and runs comfortably off the tongue.

Someone to say it to   Having an audience in its broadest sense is having someone to tell something to, not only at public performances but to a class, a group, a partner or even to one's self. It can mean a full-scale production, a school concert, an assembly, reporting back, sharing views within the group, helping younger ones with a problem, telling a story, reciting a poem, portraying a character. An audience gives purpose to an activity as well as the need to speak with clarity, audibility, to rehearse, self-criticise, and to appreciate the style and register required.

How to prepare   When we are preparing something to say in front of others we ask ourselves:

- who will I tell this to?
- how big is my audience?
- how big is the room; will they be able to hear me?
- do I know who I am talking to?
- what is my relationship to the audience?
- is my material well prepared?
- am I confident in what I have to say?

Most of these apply to children too and we need to help them to be well prepared so that they are comfortable with what they have to say (despite on-stage nerves which we all have!) and to grow in confidence with each successful presentation.

How to present it   Register and style of speech, intonation, stress, pace, clarity, whether to use Standard English (SE), dialect or an accent need to be considered as well as body language and facial expression.

How to improve presentation   Consider the following questions:
- was it said too fast?
- could they hear each word clearly?
- was my (our) voice(s) interesting to listen to?
- was the subject right for the audience?
- did it hold their attention?

Post-mortems always take place but need to be productive if they are to be useful and not just general chat or nit-picking. Children need to be encouraged to accept the criticisms of others which must also be offered in a constructive way.

Speaking, Listening and Thinking

> 'Language is, for the child, a rich and adaptable instrument for the realisation of his intentions; there is hardly any limit to what he can do with it', M.A.K. Halliday, *Explorations in the Functions of Language* (Edward Arnold 1973).

Until we have begun to master spoken language others can only guess at what we want to say and, until we are able to respond to the written word, we depend upon teachers, parents and the media for most of our knowledge. We are restricted by the experiences we are offered, by the level of our own understanding of those experiences and by the language in which they are presented to us. As we comprehend words and learn to use them we develop our concepts and ideas about objects, we begin to interpret events as they happen, relating them to past experiences and so see relationships between them and extend our ideas about the world in which we live.

The ability to be able to use spoken language freely, clearly and skilfully is referred to as oracy. It enables us to get on with others, making our ideas, intentions and needs known to them, and is a means of learning through interaction with others.

The development of oracy is central to our learning. Through listening to words in context we become familiar with their usage and bring them into our own spoken vocabulary. Our language skills help us to interpret events around us, relate them to past experiences and make connections or see relationships between them.

Most of us can speak and listen, provided we have no physical impairment, because it is part of our nature. Regrettably, the development of our spoken language skills has not been given its full weight of attention until recently.

The National Curriculum guidelines focus on the nature of spoken language for its own sake as well as its central role in the development of written language. Speaking and listening are combined (AT1) because one cannot exist without the other; they are two sides of the same coin. Speaking and listening are also an integral part of learning so are essential to the written language modes as well as separate from them.

There are three reasons why we need spoken language.

Need	Aspect	Function
someone to talk with	social	to get on with others
something to say	communicative	to transfer meaning to others
something to find out	cognitive	as a means of learning

Teacher's Notes

These reasons are not mutually exclusive; in fact, each contains an element of the other two. Children develop and use speaking and listening for these different purposes provided that they have a wide variety of contexts in which they can both actively listen and speak.

Speaking

'Children should be helped to acquire as wide as possible a range of language uses so that they can speak appropriately in different situations', Bullock, 10.6, *A Language for Life* (HMSO 1975).

Children need to talk. Not only is it cathartic, but the questioning child is the developing child. Speaking is the means by which we communicate with, and come to understand, the experience of others which we then compare with our own, so creating links between the new and the familiar.

The need to talk, to communicate, is in each and every one of us. Frustration comes when we are unsuccessful and acquire a sense of failure or inability to perform well. We need to be able to speak with confidence and in a way that the listener can comprehend. We need to engage the listener's attention by speaking in a lively and interesting way. We must stress the important words or phrases so they are retained; we have to speak at a speed which is fast enough to encourage listening but not so fast that the listener cannot keep up.

In dialogue we have to listen carefully so that our responses are pertinent to the discussion. The words we use should be ones that we know will be understood whether in dialect, accent or jargon. Decisions have to be made according to whether we want to persuade, coerce, plead, argue, comment, dismiss, laugh, or just make sounds to acknowledge that we are listening (AT1 L3-6). Above all this we need a reservoir of words that enable us to furnish what we want to say with the appropriate language (Programmes of Study for AT1).

Speaking is not just an encoding skill. We talk to:
- report experiences, past and present
- express our own ideas, thoughts, observations and opinions
- reflect and to reason
- seek or pass on information and instructions
- improve our command of spoken English and widen our vocabulary
- improve confidence and increase self-expression
- express imaginative thought
- justify actions and behaviour
- explore relationships
- communicate.

We need:
- clear speech without impediment or immaturity
- wide vocabulary
- dialogue and collaboration with others
- skills of reasoning and argument
- the ability to formulate and express ideas
- the ability to predict, hypothesise and compare alternatives.

We develop the skills through a range of activities:
- by explaining how things work, or experiments were conducted
- by recounting events and happenings and discussing findings and observations
- by telling original stories and retelling known ones
- by reading aloud our own writing and that of others
- by a range of physical and mental games
- by delivering messages
- by giving direction or instructions
- through drama and role-play
- in school assembly – leading, reading our own stories and prayers, acting
- through poetry and music, rhythm and sound patterns
- in discussion of our responses to pictures, music, poetry, plays to explore feelings and emotions
- through our own, amateur and professional paintings to give insight into others' ideas and feelings
- through pictures to help recall and to recreate events
- through using the telephone.

The aim of the *First Speaking and Listening Kit* is to provide a range of stimulating material to assist the development of these spoken language skills and provide models for speaking and listening activities.

Listening

Listening skills are not easy to define and yet children probably spend more time in school listening than using any other language mode. Listening skills need to be taught, not in isolation, but as part of an integrated approach to language development. Listening is not merely a decoding skill, it requires the listener to match the heard with the known or experienced so as to gain understanding and to develop concepts. Listening has to be *active* if the response is to be appropriate. We need to listen actively to the speaker to ascertain the purpose and context of the talk. We have to listen to the intonation, the stresses and the pace of what is said, the register and style, and break through any barriers that may be caused by dialect or accent. As we listen we are required to select from what is being said, match it with our own knowledge and make judgements in order to participate or predict according to the needs of the moment.

If the situation is non-reciprocal, e.g. listening to a radio programme or as part of an audience, judgements are made through talk inside our heads by comparing what we have heard with what we already know. In a group situation, these can be externalised, discussed and compared with those of others.

We all need time to listen to ourselves, to pause, reflect and review what we have learned, to take the opinions of others and compare them with our own or to consider how effectively we have done a particular task. There are times when it is appropriate to give children tasks to do without talking, allowing them to concentrate on their own thinking and helping them to learn to listen to themselves.

Teacher's Notes

Children need to experience as wide a spectrum of listening opportunities as possible, e.g. story, poetry, rhyme, newspaper articles, their own work, yours, visitors of all kinds, productions, TV, video and radio recordings. They need to be exposed to different kinds of music, cultural, classical, standard, pop, and to be given the opportunity to respond through words, mime, music, rhythm, movement and dance. Children also need to learn to be good audiences, to be able to share experiences, to switch on and off from humour and pathos, to dip into the make-believe world and out again, and listen to talks by an adult or child presenting first-hand experience, so adding to their store of knowledge.

We listen for pleasure and as a means of learning:
- to extract information
- to receive and follow instructions
- to build up hypotheses and develop concepts
- to learn appropriate pronunciation
- to learn the pattern and structure of language
- for communication and social interaction
- to listen to the essential content whilst ignoring distractions
- to consider another's point of view
- to educate and broaden emotional response
- to learn about others and build relationships.

We need physical attributes of:
- good auditory memory to remember sound and word patterns and to put things in sequence
- good auditory acuity to be able to hear clearly – affected by temporary deafness (catarrhal), deafness in varying degrees and in differing frequencies
- good auditory discrimination to develop fine sound awareness.

We develop skills through activities:
- by search and selective listening – to stories, music, poetry; by answering questions; through discussion and debate
- by responding correctly to verbal instructions
- by imitative listening
- by memorising poems and rhymes
- through games of word-play
- through rhyme, rhythm and sound
- through a variety of media.

Listening at all levels is vital to development at all stages but the attention span is limited; the longer the length of listening time the less effectively one listens. Active listening, i.e. listening for a purpose, increases the attention span (AT1 3c) through activities like listening to stories, asking and responding to questions, commenting on what has been said, etc. Passive listening has a limited attention span at any age. We need to get the balance right for the age and ability of our pupils because learning to talk comes through listening.

Thinking
Language and thought are not the same. Our thoughts allow us continually to re-interpret and re-organise the knowledge in our heads by assimilation and accommodation and so take on board new knowledge. Language is the means by which we reflect upon these thoughts, take responsibility for what we receive, and then remake it so that it builds on our existing knowledge base. We read newspapers, magazines, listen to the media and discuss ideas; but it is through language and thought that we accept or reject them.

Talk is not only the way we communicate with others. Language, which is audible inside our heads throughout our waking hours, commenting, interpreting, dreaming, imagining, also guides our paths and deepens the quality of thought, making sense of our lives. Language and thought may not be the same but by developing spoken language skills we are able to reach greater depths of reasoning and understanding.

The *First Speaking and Listening Kit* aims to present materials and tasks that encourage the development of active listening, confident speaking and reasoning, contributing to all aspects of spoken language.

Speaking and Listening in the Classroom

Language is the basic tool that equips children for life and it is through language that all learning takes place. A child's ability to use spoken language grows through having not only a wide variety of different things to talk about and opportunities for purposeful discussion but also a number of varied, interesting and real reasons for applying it. Activities need to relate to areas of which children have knowledge or experience, not to things they have never thought, talked of, nor heard about.

Children need opportunities for make-believe situations which they create themselves so that they can re-interpret, through action and role-play, what they know in the light of what they come to learn:
- a drama corner where domestic scenes, shopping and hairdressing can take place
- improvisations from story, poetry, rhyme and TV themes of heroes, adventurers, witches, giants and fairies fed by nursery rhymes and singing games, stories told by teachers, parents and peers, poems read, plays and media presentations.
- time for gossip.

These kind of opportunities for talk consolidate learning and provide a way of re-ordering experience which allows children to absorb it and make sense of it.

Children need to encounter situations which require them to use more elaborate forms of language through which they are motivated to extend their level of language complexity. Simply working with a sympathetic adult will not, in itself, develop more complex forms of language in children who are not accustomed to using them. Situations requiring these forms have to be created. Planned intervention assists children's language development and ensures growth if it is based on recognised needs which have been identified by effective record keeping of progress. Situations need to be 'realistic' to allow children to bring their own knowledge to bear upon the

Teacher's Notes

tasks thus giving them real meaning. The children also have a chance to get to the core of the task, to gain leverage from it, so forming relevant ideas and opinions which they can then proffer to the task or to discussion. They also need the opportunity to extend their newly acquired language skills in other situations.

We should speak correctly and appropriately at all times, but we need to guard against persistently correcting a child's spoken language against the Standard English model. If children are overly concerned about how they should say what they have to say they may well become reluctant to talk freely and so could be prevented from extending their own thinking by this concern for correctness. Usage of the correct form will come, in part, from the example we set and by putting what the children have said into a more acceptable form. Later, children can be helped to use the correct form.

Considerations of spoken language must not be limited to speaking; listening is equally important. Children need to listen at a number of levels, from the urgent and alarming, the peaceful and soothing, the requiring and instructing to the dreamy half-listening, for all sorts of reasons. They need to listen actively but with imagination, to wallow in the language of story, rhyme, poetry and imagination and let it flow over them so that it is absorbed, almost like 'osmosis', while the mind is focusing on the content.

The aim of the *First Speaking and Listening Kit* is to provide opportunities through stimulating material not only to assist the development of spoken language skills but also to provide models for speaking and listening activities.

The *First Speaking and Listening Kit* builds on the spoken language children bring to school with them. They have already developed the skills of making language work for them, to ask for, to question why, to tell of their experiences, to recount, to recall, to receive instruction, to discuss, to collaborate, to plan and to manipulate for their own ends. Many will have learned to listen and join in sharing rhymes and stories, and to use overt language to explore their role-play games. The *First Speaking and Listening Kit* provides stimulating and enjoyable activities to extend this language base in an exciting way, to develop children's discussion skills and provide realistic opportunities for group discussion.

Classroom Activities

There are many activities that are ongoing in the classroom to assist spoken language development; a kit can only support, give ideas and extend what should already be taking place.

News-time This talking together, sharing and exchanging views, is very important for the young child. It encourages them to talk in front of others while the general chatter and talk that goes on first thing in the morning, the sharing and exchanging the narrative of their lives, helps to establish a trusting atmosphere in which children matter and where they know they can make a viable contribution.

Show and tell Once children are comfortable with talking about things and sharing the story of their lives introduce Show and tell. Arrange for two or three children each day to bring to school something they care about, or have been given, or have made. Encourage them to find out as much as they can about it before they bring it to school so they have a solid foundation of information to work from. Arrange a table for the display of these treasures and have a felt pen and cards on it for making the labels. During talking time the performer talks about the treasure and during that day the children may look at and handle carefully another's precious possession.

Naming circle This game develops confidence because children are working from the known but it also reinforces possessive pronouns. Sit with the children in a circle and 'read' round. Start by turning to the neighbour on your left saying, of your right-hand neighbour, 'His/her name is . . . , my name is . . . and your name is . . .' The person on your left turns to his/her left-hand neighbour and says of you 'His/her name is . . . , my name is . . . and your name is . . .' As children become confident you can increase the number of names called.

Word-play
- Say a well-known nursery rhyme such as Jack and Jill and ask which word rhymes with 'Jill' or 'down'.
- I spy . . . a word that begins (or ends) with the same sound as 'wall'.
- Have a number of cards, each with a letter of the alphabet on it, in a bag or box, pull out one and ask for a word that begins with the same sound, or rhymes with it. Initially allow any word that fits but later refine it to sets of things (animals, colours, flowers, toys, clothes) to aid classification.
- Other ideas include: Chinese Whispers, Simon Says, The Parson's Cat, I Packed my Bag.

Directions How to get to another classroom, the Head's room, the Office, home from school, to Gran's, to a friend's house, to the local shops, etc.

Stories, poems and rhymes Sharing one's delight in stories sustains interest in reading as books grow more difficult. Telling and reading stories of worth makes meaning come alive and lights up language for children. Always study a book first to see what it has to offer the listening children. A poor story is no help to them, it does not develop their concept of story, concentration span or language growth. Be conscious of the quality of language used by the author or poet. Poetry should be learned and stories recalled or retold. The quality of recalling in a 5+ to 6+ child is indicative of later academic performance. Give children advance organisers to focus their listening, for example:
- I want you to listen to what I say/read because I want you to think about . . . Afterwards I'm going to ask you why . . .
- listen for three things that go together
- listen for words that tell you . . .
- stop part way through and ask what they think will happen because of what has happened to date in the story
- ask why they think a character behaved in a particular way and what effect this may have on the rest of the story.

These directives help children to listen with focused attention on the task or the story and increase their attention span.

Learn a number of rhymes and poems so that you can call them up on a suitable occasion: 'Do you know this poem about . . . ?' or 'I remember a rhyme about that, listen . . .'.

Maths Give a number and ask children to perform mental mathematical operations within their compass of knowledge and to give the answer at the end of the task, not after each operation, e.g. start with five, add one, take away three, add four, take away two: what number have you reached now? As children's mathematical skills develop include operations such as multiply by a given number, divide by another number, halve or double the number and increase the number of operations.

Art
- Ask the children to draw and colour a house, a park, a treasure island, etc. as you direct. Give the instructions one at a time with younger children, later give details in larger chunks.
- Draw a scene putting in details as given.
- Make an 'identikit' poster. Display results or present as a 'wanted' poster.

PE Follow instructions and directions: pretend you are . . . , stretch up as tall as you can, walk on . . . , reds on the climbing frame, blues on . . . , balance on three points and so on. Start with children standing still, they move left or right, forwards or back, according to instructions given. First give the instructions yourself then let each child have a card picked out at random from a bag or box at the beginning of the session and when you point to a child the card held is read and the class moves accordingly.

Speaking and listening are so closely interlinked that much of the time they cannot be separated, and, as the spoken word is an integral part of learning, so it occurs not only with the written language modes of reading and writing but across all areas of the curriculum. Within and across the breadth of the curriculum the more real or 'realistic' opportunities that are created for children to use language the more likely the children are to take command of it and use it well. This, too, is the objective of the *First Speaking and Listening Kit* – to help children take control of language and make it work for them.

Getting Children to Listen

Start by finding the level at which children will actively listen. Some will have come from homes where noise is constant and they have learned to switch off from listening. When you want to tell the children something you need them to be quiet and actively listen. It is no good trying to talk over their noise and expecting them to listen, understand, remember and do as you have asked; some children can but most cannot. If you shout above their noise they will become noisier and you become like the background noise they have at home. A noisy teacher makes a noisy class. We want noise, i.e. talk, but we want it to be both useful and productive.

We all have different ways of achieving quiet but a new teacher or a new class can cause difficulties. Once you have established a means of obtaining quiet the rest is simple. How you achieve it can depend on the task the children are involved in at the time. One way, with very young children, is to bring them to the carpeted area and talk quietly with them. If noisy activities are in progress start singing a song they all know with your group and the others will soon join in. When it is finished they look at you for the next one and without raising your voice you not only have their attention but you can say what you wanted to say. Clicking fingers where they join in, a flash card, or your standing or sitting in a particular place can all be signals for them to stop and listen.

Stand or sit quietly while you give your message or instruction. Young children should stop what they are doing and look at you, then you know that they are listening. Speak clearly, moderate in tone and pitch. Check that children understand what you have said and then ask them to get on quietly. Establishing good listening habits straight away with a class brings untold dividends in attention, tasks completed and the level of language growth achieved. The language used to children must be straightforward and unambiguous so that the tasks are clear to them, then they can get to the heart of the task and apply their acquired knowledge and skills.

Listening to Them

Listening is a two-way process. We need to be aware that children not only like to be talked to but listened to as well. The amount an adult listens to a child indicates the level of care they have in that child and its development. If a child is not listened to then the ability to express him or herself, to convey ideas and information, to be understood, suffers in proportion to that lack of real interest. If we do not listen to what children say freely and willingly they will clamour to be listened to come what may, even if the situation is hopeless. Improving a child's language stems from the lively interest we show in listening; ignoring a child's language deprives him or her of becoming an active participant in the linguistic act. Listening is not a passive activity. We, too, must listen actively if we are to respond to the child, ask the right questions and so stimulate the growth of language and thinking.

The importance of conversation with individuals and small groups of children cannot be over-emphasised. Claims on the teacher's time means that it is not always easy to give time to a young child who wants to share something of importance. But it is only through this close personal contact with a caring, listening adult that children's own language develops. They know that the teacher is interested in their activities and in themselves as individuals so they grow both linguistically and emotionally.

A trusting relationship between peers, or an adult and child, enables problems to be shared and talked through. Eighteen per cent of all children will be disturbed for a period of their school life. These children especially need time to talk during

Teacher's Notes

their disturbed period if they are to come through it successfully.

The more time spent listening to children as individuals or in small groups the greater their powers of listening will be and the more self-confident they will become. We must find time to listen to them: it is vitally important to their language growth and language, after all, is the foundation of all learning.

Drama

Drama is a natural development of nursery dressing-up and role-play and a vehicle for extending oral work. At Key Stage 1 opportunities should exist for drama to be developed through improvisation, role-play and enactment, responding to visual and aural stimuli, collaborative and exploratory play, imaginative play, etc.

For young children, drama is a form of play based on real, heard or imagined experience. The Home Corner satisfies their need to act out everyday situations, to clarify and organise these experiences. It is through projecting themselves into a situation that children learn to distinguish themselves from it. This is a truly educational process.

Drama, whether it be improvised or concerned with performance, asks children to adopt other roles, to move around in the skins of other people simulating the role in its response to a given situation. By putting on the mask of that person children are freed from their own inadequacies. Young children can express virtually all human emotions from laughter and joy to grief and sorrow. The areas they explore are limited only by their experience.

Apart from developing speaking and listening skills drama also
- develops confidence
- increases understanding of others and so facilitates relationships
- brings an awareness of the power of the spoken word, and the possibilities afforded by intonation, gesture, facial expression, pause
- promotes an appreciation of drama as an art form through observing and participating in performances.

Drama is present when people are coping with or solving a problem and often involves conflict of one kind or another. The conflict may be between two people or can involve the whole class. It can be imaginative or can be a way of working through a problem within the class. For example two senior citizens arguing over a favourite seat can be linked with whose seat is whose in the classroom, or who is first in line.

Roles are about attitudes and therefore children need to know a great deal about the character, its life and times. Simple masks allow the act to be important *not* the person behind it. For shy or nervous children it provides anonymity, allows them to open up and to use spoken language in a way they would not have been able to do as themselves.

Teachers need to vary the roles they take; children will accept them in role and also accept their returning to the role of teacher. When you first work on improvised drama with the whole class it can help if you take a leading role. Sort the children into groups or pairs to role-play neighbours, other householders, people in the street, policemen and possibly social workers, depending on the problem. Say that you are going out of the classroom and when you return you will be someone with a problem. While you are gone ask them to think about the kind of person they are, how they dress, stand, think, speak and behave.

When you come back in you could be very agitated because someone has left a baby, animal, parcel on your doorstep. What shall you do with it? Where shall you take it? You cannot keep it because of x, y and z reasons, or you may have lost something, or you have water coming through the ceiling, or you've come home and found an alien in your lounge!

No matter the age of the group you need a very varied collection of literature, including fairy stories which are a good source. Keep a folder for ideas because often one improvisation sparks off ideas for another or suggests ways that may work better.

We need a variety of ways of working in drama. There has to be structure or freedom cannot come into being. Rules need to be clear to give it framework. You may want to stipulate that no one must physically touch another so that words, gestures, expression, intonation form their response. Let groups show each other what they have done if it is worthy of being shared.

Drama is never finished: it always grows, develops and changes. It is an ideal vehicle for developing speaking and listening for all children.

Group Work

The value of group work means that children are not limited by their own horizons, by their own thinking or acquired knowledge and prejudices. They learn that there are other points of view and other areas of thought which they have neither known nor considered, and often reach a higher level of learning than they could have reached separately.

Group work is the focus of many of the activities in the *First Speaking and Listening Kit* because it places the control of their learning in the hands of the pupils: children have to form hypotheses and evaluate them for themselves (AT: PoS 7). By going back to the evidence in the text and studying it more closely, discussing it against their existing view of how things are, gained from their own experience of the real world, they can test these newly formed hypotheses.

The *First Speaking and Listening Kit* starts with pairs to help children learn to work together instead of alongside each other. It is also easier for young children, if they only have one other person to consider, to listen without interrupting their

Teacher's Notes

partner and to have a chance to put their own point of view.

When group activities are introduced begin with friendship groups because children speak more confidently among friends (just as we do) and this helps to get discussion going. Once they are working productively, or if you find familiarity with each other produces the opposite – as it sometimes can – vary the groups, choose them randomly, or according to working sets, topic group or groups chosen by you because of your knowledge of how your pupils work – the meek ones, the dominant ones, those that need their wild statements challenged or those who need to be stretched. Ability groups allow children to pit their skills against one another in a different way without intimidating (albeit unwittingly) meeker or less able children. You can then work with a 'quiet' group encouraging the children to speak up with less anxiety. Working with single sex groups in curriculum areas such as science, technology or computer work permits girls to reach results as quickly and efficiently as boys in areas that have tended to be male-dominated, without being pushed aside by boys, put down or expected to assume a less than equal status (AT: PoS 7).

After reaching their conclusions the group can choose a spokesperson to report back to the class. Reporting back can push a group forward by opening their eyes to different aspects of the subject, by making new or different demands on accuracy or on the need to be more explicit, or to tighten up on the way they have organised the structure of their task.

Assessment

> 'The assessment of speaking and listening should, where possible, be informal, continuous and incidental, applied to tasks carried out for curricular purposes', *English from 5 to 16* (HMSO 1990).

Assessment of listening is based on what children say or do in response to what they have heard. By observing talk teachers gain insights into how children interact with each other, what they know and how they think, thereby judging the quality of what children say rather than their vociferousness. 'Good' talk may be simple in linguistic structure or in vocabulary but it should be pertinent, showing comprehension of the task and an understanding of the purpose and audience to which it is addressed.

It can be difficult to assess children's progress in spoken language because it is dependent upon many factors – the audience, the task, the knowledge the children bring to the task, their experience of oral work, their fluency with the language, their self-confidence, motivation, gender, emotional state in relation to what they bring to school and to the task, and the atmosphere in which assessment is taking place.

Children need to be observed across a number of different tasks and working situations to make a fair assessment of their effective use of language. Spoken language is concerned with someone to talk to (social interaction), something to say (communication) and something to find out (cognition). If we keep to these three elements we can make a holistic, interactional approach to assessment rather than an analytical one.

Writing down exactly what children say about their drawings in the way they say it, dating and keeping these on a regular basis is evidence in one area. Reporting back from group discussions can indicate the depth of discussion which has taken place, indicate whether a group is moving forward and identify which ones need closer observation to provide further evidence for recording purposes. Day-to-day classroom activities, stories, games, following instructions and directions, taking messages, etc., all add to and form part of the whole.

By making both formal and informal observations throughout the year, by having samples of actual talk and by recording responses to open-ended questions you will have evidence of the progress a child has made with you. One way of recording assessment would be to note the Attainment Target statement and record the task undertaken, the related copymaster(s) and the date.

Name: Charley Blank		d.o.b. 19.1.87	
Level	Statement	Sheet no./Task	Date
2 a)	Participate as speakers and listeners in a group engaged in a given task	9 : Small group took active part in discussion on Wishing	1.7.92

If we ensure that the activities we structure for children allow them to grow in the areas of speaking and listening, then recording by observation, noting utterances that show growth in these areas and by using a tape recorder, video or camcorder to supplement notes, we will be able to show evidence of that growth.

The activities in the *First Speaking and Listening Kit* allow this to happen and can be used to give evidence of progress and to identify the National Curriculum areas covered by the children.

A teacher's assessment copymaster linking the activity sheets with the levels of the National Curriculum can be found at the end of the book.

Using the Sheets

Materials
For most of the activities, children will need access to rough paper for making notes, lead pencils, coloured pencils or felt-tip pens, scissors and glue or paste.

Teacher's Notes

Discussion
Much of the work at Levels 1 and 2 will be done through oral work in the day-to-day activities common to the infant classroom. Many of the early activity sheets will support this approach and can be used as class activities (e.g. **Who are You?**) or in groups, with help, in the early stages.

Spend a few minutes talking about an activity to prepare the children. This preliminary discussion will focus the children's minds and begins to point up issues. It will also ensure that children understand the task and highlight words they do not understand.

Children will work in groups of four to six members, in pairs and also alone to prepare for a group activity.

Who Goes First?
Two ways of deciding who goes first would be:
1. Provide each group with a die. The groups elect either the highest or the lowest number to go first. Each has a throw. Any two numbers the same means that those children have another throw to determine their place.
2. Go alphabetically by their first names. If any two names begin with the same letter use their surname or the second letter of their first name to determine who precedes the other.

Group Task
Once the children are busily working in groups or pairs, go from group to group, listening in and moving them on if they are stuck. You may need to work with younger or slower groups for a time.

Follow Up
Bring the children back together at the end of an activity so that they can share opinions and views. In some cases suggestions are made for specific follow up activities but there are many other ways of extending the task other than those given. The sheets are not an end in themselves. They can be a jumping off point for a whole field of study and become a topic in themselves.

Presentation
Children should listen attentively to what others are saying. When expressing their views and opinions, they should be helped to make their comments clear, cogent, pointing up main issues in the argument or debate, and free from repetitive rambling. Children should be encouraged to make their responses brief and to the point.

Reading aloud should be in a clear voice, its tone suited to the passage. When role-playing, words should be spoken in a clear, carrying voice and suited to the part in tone and accent.

Children should be encouraged to present any written work to be displayed in the best possible way, with clear handwriting, good spelling and appropriate punctuation. The work should be attractively mounted or framed. As an alternative to mounting, try one of these ideas: use felt pens to draw a line to frame the writing; draw a picture in one corner, or faintly behind the writing; make a border.

Booklets
The result of discussions can make interesting reading. Make a display of their comments or put them in a booklet. The finished booklets should be readily available and become part of the class's reading material enabling a topic to be discussed long after the activity is concluded.

There are a number of ways to make booklets but here is a quick one. Place A4 sheets inside a piece of thin card, staple down the centre and fold to make booklets for immediate use. Make sure the sharp ends of the staples are on the inside so the spine remains smooth. The front cover should be attractively designed and the title easy to read. Children's work can be pasted inside using frames and illustrations to make the pages attractive. Use crayons rather than felt-tip pens so that colour does not 'bleed' through the paper.

If the activity becomes part of a topic, make a quality book with hard covers, stitched pages and a hessian spine.

Notes on the Use of Each Sheet

Who Lives Here?

Materials   One copymaster sheet per pair, scissors, glue and felt-tips.

Class task   Discussion: Ask the children if they have visited a farm and discuss the animals they may have seen. Talk about the pets they may have. Are the animals the same? Give out the sheets. Talk about the animals, ask where they live.

Pairs task   Instructions: Cut out the animals and stick them on to the correct picture.

Follow up   Class activity: Make a graph about the children's pets and discuss information obtained from it. You could go on a farm visit and compare the animals found there with those on the copymaster.

Asim Wants a Biscuit

Materials   One copymaster sheet per pair or group.

Class task   Discussion: Talk about times when they have tried to reach something too high for them. What did they do? Write 'What happened?' on the board as you ask the question. Give out the sheets.

Group or pairs task   Instructions: What was Asim trying to do? How did he make himself taller? What happened to Asim and the biscuits? Why? Go through the text with the children and work with any group having difficulty.

Follow up   Class activity – reporting back: Bring together and ask each group to report back. Keep a note of any group there was not time for so that they have first chance next time. Aspects of safety in the home can be discussed in this context.

Teacher's Notes

Where is my Home?

Materials   Scissors, one copymaster sheet per pair.

Class task   Discussion: Where do animals live? Explain that the task is to find the right home for each of the creatures.

Pairs task   Instructions:
1. Cut out the cards and match them.
2. Play pelmanism (memory game). Place the cards face down. Decide who goes first. The first child picks up two cards, in this case one long and one short. They read the cards aloud. If a correct match has been made they keep the cards, if not the cards are placed face down in their original position. The winner of a pair has another go. The cards can be played both ways, e.g. 'I am a spider. My home is a web.' or 'My home is a web. I am a spider.'

Follow up   Pairs activity: Children can add to the game by devising more cards from their own knowledge base.

Who are You?

Materials   Scissors, paper or cloth bag, one copymaster sheet per group.

Preparation   Play miming games like 'Let's pretend'. First of all, you mime a person doing a task and ask the children to guess who you are. Only say 'yes' or 'no' in response to their questions.

Class task   Invite a volunteer and whisper in the child's ear the character to be mimed. Remind them that they can only say 'yes' or 'no'. Ask the kind of questions that extract information so that children have experience of the kinds of questions they can ask.

Discussion: Remind children of the miming games you have played and divide the class into groups. Provide each group with a cloth or paper bag.

Group task   Instructions: Cut along the lines, fold each card and put it in the bag provided. Each member of the group takes it in turns to take out a card and mime the occupation. Go from group to group listening to their questioning.

Follow up   Group activity: Devise a set of cards based on well-known characters from nursery rhymes or stories.

What's the Message?

Materials   Pencil, rough paper and felt-pens, one copymaster sheet per pair.

Class task   Discussion: Give out the sheets and go through the first task with the children. Talk about the scene and write their suggestions for what might be said on the board, forming two columns to correspond with the pictures. Discuss each one and help them to decide which is the most suitable.

Pairs task   Firstly they copy the agreed statement on the first picture. Then they follow the same procedure with number two, writing their ideas in rough, selecting the most suitable, writing it on the sheet and colouring in the picture.

Follow up   Pairs activity: Ask each pair to devise a story of their own and exchange it with another pair's to work out. They can discuss the responses and consider how close the others came to their original story plan.

What am I?

Materials   One copymaster sheet per pair, scissors.

Class task   Discussion: Encourage children to describe a creature they have seen. What does it look like? How is it the same as other creatures? How is it different from others? Explain that the task is to match the right description to each of the creatures.

Pairs task   Instructions:
1. Cut out the cards and match them.
2. Play the memory game. If children do not remember how to play pelmanism, remind them. The cards can be played both ways, e.g. 'I am a tiger. I can run. I have stripes.' or 'I can run. I have stripes. I am a tiger.'

Follow up   Pairs activity: Children can add to the game by devising more cards from their own knowledge base. They could also devise a set of inanimate objects (aeroplane, car, computer, etc.) and give their corresponding functions.

Sorting and Setting 1

Materials   One copymaster sheet per pair or group, large sheets of paper and lengths of ribbon, string or tape and paper clips for making sets. Ensure that there are sufficient objects for this task within the classroom.

Preparation   Give children experience of sorting objects into a range of categories.

Class task   Using the photocopied sheets ask children to describe the objects in the sets. What do they have in common? Why are some objects in the middle: what does that mean?

Pairs or group task   Instructions: Choose a colour – red or blue and a shape – square or round. Find things that are the colour and the shape. Also find things that have both attributes. Draw the sets and label them. Suggest that children bring suitable objects from home, after obtaining their parents' permission.

Follow up   Pairs or group task: Select a miscellany of objects of their own choosing but with two dissimilar attributes to make into sets.

Story Board

Materials   Pencil, rough paper, one copymaster sheet per pair.

Class task   Discussion: Talk about something that happened to you but do not say how it ended. Ask children to suggest what could have happened. Encourage them to justify their responses. Ask them to tell the class or group things that have happened to them but to leave out the ending for others to guess.

Teacher's Notes

Pairs or small group task Instructions:
1. Talk about what has happened to Jenny and think of the different ways this story could end. Choose the one that suits the story best and draw or write it down.
2. Now do the same with the story of Zip. Did he get his football in the end? How?

Follow up Each group designs a story board and exchanges with another group to devise the ending for the story. Later the two groups can join together to discuss whether the ending is the one originally thought of or whether the new ending is more appropriate.

Wishing

Materials Pencil and rough paper. One copymaster sheet per pair.

Class task Talk about wishes. What are they? Do they come true?

Pairs task Instructions: Read through the sheet with the children but do not discuss it with them because it might influence what they say. If a group is having difficulty join in to get them started.

Follow up Class discussion: Bring the class together and have an open debate on wishes and wishing. Ask them about the wishes they have made and the reasons for their choices.

Choices

Materials One copymaster sheet per group.

Class instructions Give the children five minutes or so to talk about all the different things they can find in Santa's workshop before moving them on to the full task.

Group task Instructions: Read through the sheet with the children. Encourage them to work from memory – attempting to record may inhibit the child's choices.

Follow up Class discussion: Bring children together to talk about their choices. Choices, like wishing, can tell us so much about the children themselves, their thoughts and their concerns.

Question and Answer

Materials Scissors, one copymaster sheet per pair. Have a selection of resource books and cards on display for children to research the topics.

Class task Discussion: Encourage children to describe different creatures and their natural habitats.

Pairs task Instructions:
1. Cut out the cards and find the right location for each of the creatures.
2. Play pelmanism (see **Where is my Home?**).

Follow up Pairs task: Children can either
1. Add to the game by devising more cards from their own knowledge base.
2. Choose one of the animals and find out more about it.

My Giant Sandwich

Materials One copymaster per pair.

Preparation Play games like 'In my Christmas stocking I had . . .', 'I went to the supermarket and I bought . . .'

Group task Instructions: Play the game 'In my giant sandwich I had a . . .' Each member of the group says the first item and adds another. Try to go round the group twice.

Follow up Group activity: The group could make a painting, a collage, or a model of their giant sandwich with junk or clay.

Class task Discussion: Continue the theme with the rhyme 'One man went to mow . . . One man and his dog and a packet of crisps . . .' Add a man and a portion of food each time.

I Didn't Mean To . . .

Materials Pencil, glue, felt pens and rough paper.

Class task Discussion: Talk about familiar stories, e.g. Goldilocks, Cinderella, The Three Little Pigs. Take them through the story stage by stage. Help them to condense each stage into one sentence and write that sentence on a chalk board or flip chart. Discuss the story as a whole, how one stage leads to another.

Pairs task Instructions: Firstly the children should cut out the four pictures and discuss the order in which to stick them on to the story board. How might this story start? What could happen next? Which picture tells the end of the story? After gluing down the picture the children should work on one part of the story at a time. Tell them to start with the first picture. What might the children be saying about the football? Ask them to write their ideas in rough. When they are satisfied with the first part of their story they can write it on the sheet and proceed to picture two.

Follow up Class discussion:
1. The groups may like to read out their stories to the class. Discuss together how they were treated. Look for similarities and differences. Could the stories have been improved in any way?
2. Discuss the children's behaviour; could the damage have been avoided? How? What might they do another time?
3. Children can create their own story board using large sheets of paper so that the stories can be wall-mounted for others to read.

Working on stories in this way will enable children to see that each part of a story is important to the whole and must have its own weight. This will be helpful when writing their own stories. It also helps to get them thinking about their social responsibilities.

Teacher's Notes

Caged

Materials   One copymaster sheet per pair.

Class task   Discussion: Talk about things they like to do and how they feel when they are prevented from doing them (as an awareness-raising activity but not to pre-empt the task).

Pairs task   Instructions: Read through the copymaster sheet but do not discuss the questions. Allow the children between five and ten minutes to talk about them.

Follow up   Class discussion:
1. Bring the class back together and let them share the results of their discussions.
2. Make a wall picture of a creature in a cage and ask each group to write down their opinions using a strip of paper for each one. Glue them around the cage.
3. On another occasion discuss other caged animals, e.g. pets like budgies, rabbits. Would it be safe to let a caged animal loose into the wild, i.e. its natural habitat? Why do some animals need to be rescued from the wild and put into custody of some sort?

Word Wall Puzzle

Materials   Scissors, glue, paper, one copymaster per pair.

Class task   Discussion: Create a story of up to five short sentences with the children on a large sheet of paper. Cut up each one and give to a group to remake into the original story.

Pairs task   Instructions: Tell the children to cut off only one row at a time; each alternate row makes a sentence. As they complete a sentence they must stick it down on a separate sheet. Ask them how they will know which is the first word and which is the last word of the sentence.

Follow up   Children can make up a short story of their own or copy one from a book for their partner, or another pair, to remake.

Party Time

Materials   One copymaster sheet per pair, pencils, felt-pens, rough paper.

Class task   Discussion: Talk about parties the children have had or been to. What do they think goes into the preparations for a party?

Pairs or group task   Instructions:
1. Decide why the children are having a party (birthday, Christmas, etc.), when to hold the party and what is needed in the form of drinks, eats, games and who they wish to invite.
2. Design an invitation card for the party. Decide what needs to go on to it so the guests will be able to get to the party.

Follow up   Class activity: Plan a class party – for end of term, end of topic, helpers' thank-you party, feast-day, etc. Design invitations for special guests.

The Wind and the Sun

Materials   One copymaster per pair or group. Lengths of suitable fabric or garments in the dressing up box to clothe the wind and the sun. Children can use their own coats to enact the man. Have ready, for afterwards, the fable of the North Wind and the Sun by Fontaine.

Pairs or group task   Instructions: Read the text of the sheet through with the class to make sure they understand the words and the nature of the task. Encourage groups to perform their playlets to the class.

Class activity   Discussion: How similar were the playlets? Read Fontaine's story; choose a version with atmospheric pictures (e.g. Brian Wildsmith). How close were their versions to his story? Do they agree with Fontaine that the sun would be more effective?

Follow up   Children could practise their playlets and perform them to other classes.

My Home

Materials   One copymaster sheet per pair, pencils and paper.

Class task   Discussion: Talk about the different kinds of homes that people live in and the things in them that are important to them – special toys, books, rooms, clothes, mementoes, treasures of different kinds, their family.

Pupil task   Instructions:
1. Draw their own home and put in the picture all the things that matter to them.
2. Join with a partner and take it in turns to tell them about the things in the picture and why they are there.
3. Talk about the things that are the same and the things that are different in both pictures. Discuss why there are similarities and differences.

Follow up   Make a display of their 'home' pictures.

Favourite Things

Materials   Pencil and one copymaster sheet per pair.

Class task   Discussion: Talk about the children's favourite things and why they are special.

Pairs task   Instructions:
1. Write their name in the first space and fill in their favourite colour, food and toy.
2. Write down their partner's name in the second space and ask for their choices.
3. Talk about why they are their favourite things.
4. Fill in the rest of the blanks with the choices of others in the class.
5. Discuss the similarities and differences.

Follow up   Class activity: Talk with the class about their findings. Make a class graph using these charts to extract the preferences of each member of the class. See how these compare with individual charts and talk about the differences between them.

Teacher's Notes

Goldilocks and the Three Bears

Materials   One copymaster per pair. Paper plates, felt pens, oddments of wool, material and glue for the faces. Use old rulers, stiff card or wood strips to make the handles.

Preparation   Working with paper bag puppets and glove puppets, or a visit from a puppeteer will help children to feel confident in this task.

Class task   Discussion: Go through the story of Goldilocks with the children. Ask them who the characters are and to say what happens. If something is missed out ask 'Is that what happened next?'

Group task   Instructions:
1. Choose which character each member of the group will create. Make it look as much like the character as possible.
2. Go through the story and practise it several times so that pupils know what their character will say and do.

Follow up   Class activity:
1. Put a big sheet over a table to make a puppet stage. The class can watch each group's performance.
2. Invite another class in to be the audience.
3. Why not have a puppet show near the end of the day and invite parents in to the performance?

Finding Out

Materials   Have ready one copymaster sheet per pair away from the test site. Have available, on a table beside the water tank, items such as a stone, a screw, some balsa wood, a bucket, a strainer, a quoit, a coin, the inside of a match box, a plastic tennis racket, two bottles – one with a top screwed on tightly, the other without a top.

Preparation   Provide opportunities for water-play so that children have experience of objects floating and sinking. Set up a water tank and a table with the objects listed. Each pair collects a copymaster sheet from a storage wallet to take to the task. Put up a list of the items on the table.

Pairs task   Instructions:
1. Talk about what is happening in the picture.
2. Make a list of the items they are going to test and tick the column on their chart stating whether they think each will float or sink.
3. Test the item and tick the result.
4. Were their guesses proved correct? If not, why do they think it was different?

Follow up   Class activity:
1. Talk to the children about the conclusions they have drawn from this experiment.
2. Ask them to make something that will float out of paper, card and/or wood. Set up a test and time the flotation. Which group's model floated the longest? Why?

Mystery Parcel

Materials   One copymaster per pair or group. Art materials for follow up task.

Class task   Discussion: Talk about receiving parcels. How do they feel when they open one? Do they like to know what will be inside them or do they like it to be a surprise? Do they ever get parcels other than at birthdays or Christmas?

Pair or group task   Instructions:
1. Who is the parcel for?
2. What could be inside it?
3. Each one has to think what they would like to find inside the parcel and take it in turns to tell the group. The members of the group can ask why they chose that item.

Follow up   Class activity:
1. Talk about their choices of gifts. Does a pattern emerge?
2. Just for fun. Talk about all the unusual ways they could use the box.
3. Draw or paint what they would turn their box into, or provide a box to work on.

Spot the Changes

Materials   One copymaster per pair, coloured pencil, paper and pencil.

Class task   Discussion: Take two children who are alike or similarly dressed and look for the differences. Draw a square and a rectangle. Ask children to say what is different about them. Do the same with two flowers, each with a different number of petals; a four-pointed star and a five-pointed one, etc.

Pairs task   Instructions:
1. Give out sheets and talk about the differences between the two pictures.
2. Draw a ring around the things that are different.

Follow up   Class activity: Talk about the changes they found. Discuss the conclusions they have come to about the changes.

What am I Looking At?

Materials   One copymaster, a tray and a miscellany of objects made of different substances, per group.

Class task   Discussion: Ask children to pair up and find objects to put on your tray. Discuss with them the different properties of the objects, e.g. shape, colour, texture, substance, natural or man-made. *Game 1*: You think of an object on the tray and they ask questions about its properties, e.g. 'Is it made of metal?' If the answer is 'no' then all the metal objects are removed from the tray.

Teacher's Notes

Group task   Instructions:
1. Make a collection for their tray.
2. One person thinks of an object on the tray and the others ask questions to find out what it is. The 'thinker' may only answer 'yes' or 'no'. The thinker removes the eliminated objects.
3. The one who guesses correctly is the next 'thinker'.

Follow up   Class activity: Discuss the kinds of questions the children asked. Which ones proved to be good ones for reaching a speedy result?

Group activity: *Game 2*: As *Game 1* but the objects remain on the tray and the children have to remember the questions asked. *Game 3*: Put a limit on the number of questions that can be asked.

Guess What!

Materials   A variety of objects behind a screen. A large cardboard box with a side cut away makes a good screen. A copymaster for each group.

Class task   Discussion: During talking time ask a child to bring you an object. Talk with the children about it. From their statements select five things to describe but not name the object nor give away what it is. Do this a couple of times, then ask different children to have a go at making the five statements themselves.

Class task   Instructions: Put a number of objects behind a screen and say five things about one of the objects but do not name it. The children have to guess what you are thinking about and you may only answer 'yes' or 'no'. Ask for a volunteer or select someone to be behind the screen. Make sure they can be seen over the screen.

Group task   Instructions:
1. Each member of the group throws a die. If two throw the same number they throw again.
2. The highest number becomes the first 'thinker', then the next highest and so on until all the group have been behind the screen.

Follow up   Class or group activity: Place a few objects in a bag and invite a child to describe something s/he can feel without taking it out of the bag. The class tries to guess what it is, then the 'feeler' takes it out of the bag to see how accurate they were.

Telephone Talk 1

Materials   Paper and pencil, one copymaster per group.

Class task   Discussion: Talk about what is happening in the pictures. Check for any words they may not understand.

Group task   Instructions:
1. Talk about all the reasons they can think of for using the telephone, fun reasons as well as real or serious ones.
2. Work in pairs. Make up a telephone conversation and perform it to the group when it is ready.

Follow up   Class activity:
1. Talk about the reasons children have given for making a telephone call.
2. Ask each group to perform one of their telephone plays to the class.

Poems We Like

Materials   A plentiful supply of poetry books and poetry cards, one copymaster per pair.

Preparation   Always have a poem on display for children to illustrate, talk about, write about, learn, rewrite themselves in a similar style or on the same topic.

Pairs task   Instructions: Read the sheet through with the children before they start the task, check with any who might feel concerned about the text or the task.

Follow up   Class activity: Have a time for poetry session where children present the poems they have learned by heart to the class. Ask for volunteers for these sessions. Less confident children may like to work in pairs at first. Keep the sessions short.

This activity can be used on many occasions with children of different ages.

Toy Shop

Materials   Paper and pencil, one copymaster per pair or group.

Class task   Discussion: Play Kim's Game (some children may have learned this at Beavers, Brownies or Rainbow Clubs). Start with a few items, say five, covered on a tray and build up to twenty. Remove the cover for a minute or two then cover the tray again and ask the children to recall the items. Discuss ways of remembering the objects, like putting them into categories, so making it easier to remember the items. Next time you play the game remind the children of the technique but let them suggest ways of categorising the objects.

Pairs or group task   Instructions:
1. Look at the different kinds of toys in the picture. Talk about ways of remembering.
2. After two minutes turn the paper over and make a list of the toys they can remember.
3. If they are really stuck they may have one quick look.

Follow up   Class activity: Talk about the number of toys they remembered and discuss ways in which they categorised them.

Our Senses

Materials   One copymaster per pair or group, pencils.

Class task   Discussion: Discuss things we like to see, hear, etc., and things we can find out by using other senses if one is missing. Set up a touch, smell or taste display and blindfold the 'tester'.

Teacher's Notes

Pairs or group task   Instructions:
1. Talk about the picture on the sheet with a partner.
2. What would we see, hear, touch, taste and smell if we were that child?

Follow up   Class activity: Discuss with the children what they found out from the picture. Use the opportunity to talk about touching: good touching and bad touching; how it makes you feel; what to do if you do not like it; how to cope with touching that you do not like or someone asks you to keep secret.

Our Senses – Likes and Dislikes

Things we like

Materials   One copymaster per pair or group, pencil and rough paper.

Class task   Discussion: Talk about words to describe things, e.g. the rain, a treasure, their favourite food. Encourage them to use words that really tell what they like about it, e.g. sparkling, shiny, tasty, soft, cold, sweet, pretty, crisp. If they use words which are a comment rather than a description, e.g. good, ask them what is 'good' about it and use a substitute word. Write on the chalk board, or a card, words to avoid like good, great, terrific, brilliant.

Pairs or group task   Instructions:
1. Talk about things they like to see and why. Write them in the 'see' column with a 'telling' adjective.
2. Do the same for the other four senses.

Things we do not like

Class task   Discussion: Again, talk about things they do not like, discuss some of the descriptive words they use, e.g. hate – what is hateful about it? Use another word instead. Words to avoid are awful, terrible, horrid, hateful, boring. Words to use could be slimy, slithery, sharp, bitter, sour, rough, etc.

Pairs or group task   Instructions:
1. Talk about things they do not like to see and write them in the 'see' column. Use a descriptive word so that we know why they do not like it.
2. Do the same with the other four senses.

Follow up   Class activity: Discuss the things they liked and disliked and be very complimentary about interesting or unusual phrases: 'I really liked the words you used when you said . . . they helped me to understand why you liked/disliked it'. Say the phrase two or three times, 'roll it round your mouth and taste it on your tongue', as Rosemary Sutcliff would say. Help them see why you enjoy the phrase and how it makes you feel.

Calamity Kitchen

Materials   One copymaster per group.

Class task   Discussion: What do they think the word 'calamity' means? Tell of a time when you had one of those days where everything went wrong. Ask them if they have days like that.

Group task   Instructions: Talk about all the things that are happening in the picture, are about to happen or could happen.

Follow up   Class activity: Draw the groups together and talk about their findings. What different things did they find? What were the potential dangers? How could they have been avoided?

Choosing Colours

Materials   One copymaster each, pencil and rough paper.

Class task   Discussion:
1. Discuss all the different words for a colour, e.g. red; think of its shades, tones and descriptive words like 'raspberry'.
2. Go through the sheet with the children and check that they are confident with the task.
3. Work through a similar web with the children before they work on their own.

Pairs or group task   Instructions:
1. Talk about their favourite colours, which one they like best of all and why.
2. Each writes on their own chart the colours they would choose for the items mentioned. They can draw more circles if necessary.
3. Talk to their group about their colour web.

Follow up   Class activity: Display their webs either as they are or let them re-draw them on a big sheet of paper and stick on pictures to illustrate their choices.

Colours – Warm or Cool

Materials   One copymaster per pair, paint (already mixed), sheets of kitchen paper, A3 or larger.

Class task   Talk about things that make one feel warm or cool; encourage the use of descriptive phrases to help form images in the mind.

Pairs task   Instructions:
1. Talk about warm colours of fire, heat and summer.
2. Talk about cool colours of snow, ice, winter, water, trees and sky.
3. Make a chart of these colours using the copymaster.
4. Fold a piece of paper in half, open it out and 'puddle' warm colours on the fold.
5. Fold over and smooth out with their hands then open out and see what has happened.
6. Do the same with cool colours and talk about the paintings.

Follow up   Discuss the children's art work and the images made. What conclusions did they come to by comparing their warm symmetrical designs with the cool ones? Display the paintings and ask the children to write a piece about them and mount it with their paintings. Do the same with bright colours and dull colours.

Teacher's Notes

Colours for Reasons

Materials One copymaster per pair or group, coloured pencils or felt-pens.

Class task Discussion: Choose a couple of diverse things from the sheet. What are their colours? Why do they think these colours were chosen?

Pairs or group task Instructions:
1. Talk about the colour of the things in the top group of pictures. Colour them in.
2. Which colour is used for the signs in the bottom picture. Why is this colour used?
3. Colour in the pictures accordingly.

Follow up Class activity:
1. Discuss what the items have in common. What are the purpose and reasons for the colours? Are the reasons all the same?
2. Could these items be sorted to indicate this?
3. Discuss the colour for danger and why it is used. Why is it also the best colour for cars?

Sorting and Setting 2

Materials Two copymasters per pair or group, scissors, pencil and paper.

Class task Discussion: Talk about the task and words they might not be familiar with.

Pair or group task Instructions:
1. Talk about the objects in the pictures and what they know about them, e.g. what they are made from, how they are used.
2. Cut out the pictures and sort them into sets to show what they are made from. Stick the sets on to a large sheet of paper and label them.
3. Cut up the second sheet and sort into different sets, stick them down and label these new categories.

Follow up Class activity: Make a display of the different ways in which the children have sorted the universal set but only put one kind of sorting on any one sheet, e.g. what it is made from, its usage.

Birthday Wheel

Materials One copymaster per pair, pencil and rough paper.

Preparation The idea of a wheel helps children to see the cyclic nature of the calendar and the months in relation to each other. Make sure the children know which is their birthday month.

Pairs task Instructions:
1. Talk about things that happen in different months of the year. Suggest things they could find out like the longest and shortest day, festivals, saints' days, feast days, special birthdays. Try to find something for every month and write it on the wheel.
2. Collect the birth months of the class on rough paper and then write them in the correct boxes.
3. Talk about the things they can find out from their chart.

Follow up Class activity:
1. Discuss what they have found out from their research.
2. Ask how they could record the information so that it would be useful; talk about the kinds of graphs they could make.
3. Make a graph with them and talk about how the information drawn from the graph could be presented in other ways.

Work

Materials One copymaster per group.

Class task Discussion: Discuss what they think work is. Talk about the ways adults work for their living.

Group task Instructions:
1. Talk about the different kinds of work they can see people doing in the picture.
2. Talk about the good things about the job and the bad things.
3. Discuss what work they would like to do when they are grown up. Tell the group what it is that appeals to them about the job.

Follow up Class activity: Draw groups together and talk about what they would like to do. What skills will they need to acquire in order to do that job?

Sound Words

Materials One copymaster per pair or group, pencil and paper. Book making materials.

Class task Discussion: Talk about how we can make sounds using mouth, hands and feet as instruments. Use sounds made with different parts of the body to accompany songs and rhymes.

Pairs task Instructions:
1. Make a chart of the sounds made just using our mouths or hands or feet.
2. Make a book of all the sound words they can think of – happy, sad, nasty, animal, music, school, house, traffic, weather, people sounds. Use a different page for each sound. Some words will be used on more than one page.

Follow up Class activity:
1. Share the mouth, feet and hand sounds children have thought of.
2. Make a display of the books they have made for others to share.

Teacher's Notes

Telephone Talk 2

Materials   One copymaster sheet per pair, telephones, real or toy. Ask parents, the local telephone company or industry for old ones.

Class task   Discussion:
1. Before the children start the task enact a scene where a child is ringing home to ask if s/he may stay at a friend's house for tea. Play both parts yourself or invite either a parent, student or classroom aide or prime one of your most confident and able pupils to help out.
2. Tell the story of Cinderella and enact a scene where Cinderella is trying to persuade one of the Ugly Sisters to allow her to go to the ball but make it a telephone conversation.

Pairs task   Instructions:
1. Choose one of the scenes and each play one of the characters. Try to persuade the other one to change his/her mind.
2. Do the same with another scene.
3. Prepare the one you like best to perform to the class.

Follow up   Class activity: Bring the groups together and ask each one for a presentation of the scene they feel they do best.

What's it all About?

Materials   One copymaster per group.

Class task   Discussion: Discuss feelings and moods, the things that affect us and how the mood we are in affects others.

Group task   Instructions:
1. Talk about what is happening in the picture. What is the matter with the little girl? Why is she feeling like this?
2. Each one think of a different reason why.
3. Think about who would help her and how.
4. Choose a spokesperson for the group to present their views.

Follow up   Class activity:
1. Bring the groups together to hear their conclusions and discuss them.
2. What is their responsibility towards a lonely or unhappy child?

Owning Up

Materials   One copymaster per pair or group.

Class task   Discussion: Discuss how they feel when they have done something wrong.

Pair or group task   Instructions:
1. Look at the first picture then the two options. Talk about which is the right course of action and why.
2. Is it always easy to do what they know is the right thing?

Follow up   Class activity:
1. Bring the groups together and discuss the conclusions they have reached and the reasons why. Do the groups agree with each other? If not, why not?
2. Is it easy to do the right thing like owning up? How do they feel when they have done it?
3. Do they want to talk about a time when they didn't and how they felt then? What do they feel about it now?

What do you Know?

Materials   One copymaster per pair or group.

Preparation   Without making any comment as to why they might be included just ascertain that children understand all the items present in the picture.

Pair or group task   Instructions: Go through the text on the sheet, making sure that pupils understand the questions. Leave them to explore their 'new place' in pairs or small groups.

Follow up   Bring the pairs or groups together and discuss their conclusions.

Who Lives Here? 1

20

Asim Wants a Biscuit 2

Look!
  What happened to Asim?
  How did it happen?

Talk about
  Why did he do it?
  Was Asim being sensible?
  What should he have done?

Where is my Home?   3

I am a spider.	I live in the sea.
I am a fish.	I live in a pond.
I am a duck.	My home is a stable.
I am a pig.	A hive is my home.
I am a horse.	I live in a sty.
I am a cow.	My home is a web.
I am a bee.	I live in a field.
I am a bird.	A tree is where I live.

Who are You? 4

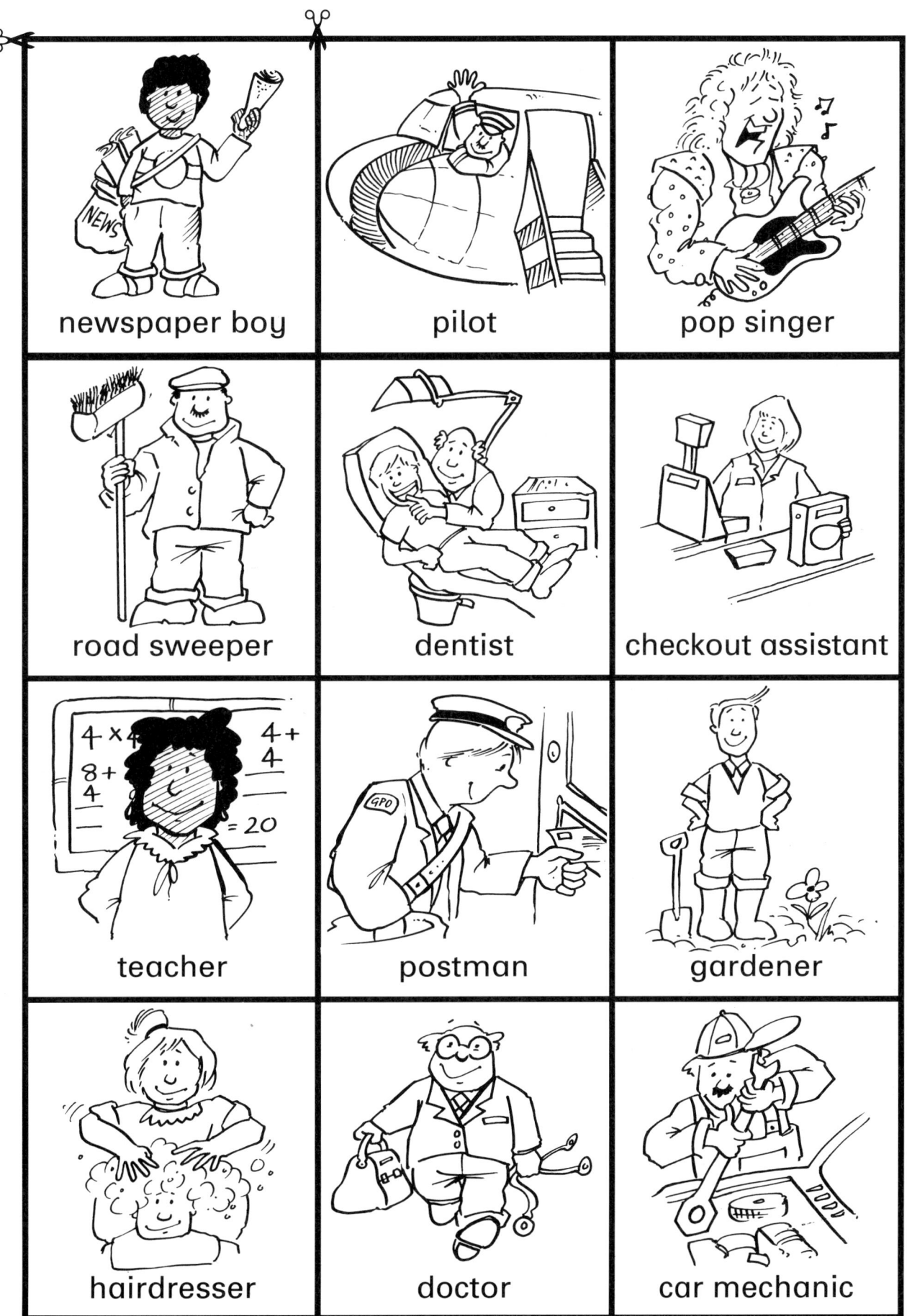

What's the Message? 5

What do you think the people are saying?

What am I?

6

I can fly. I have pretty wings.	I am a tadpole.
I can run. I have stripes.	I am a dragonfly.
I can fly. I have soft feathers.	I am a tiger.
I can run. I have a woolly coat.	I am a sheep.
I can swim. I am shiny and slippery.	I am a bird.
I can swim. I am black and wriggly.	I am a fish.

Sorting and Setting 1

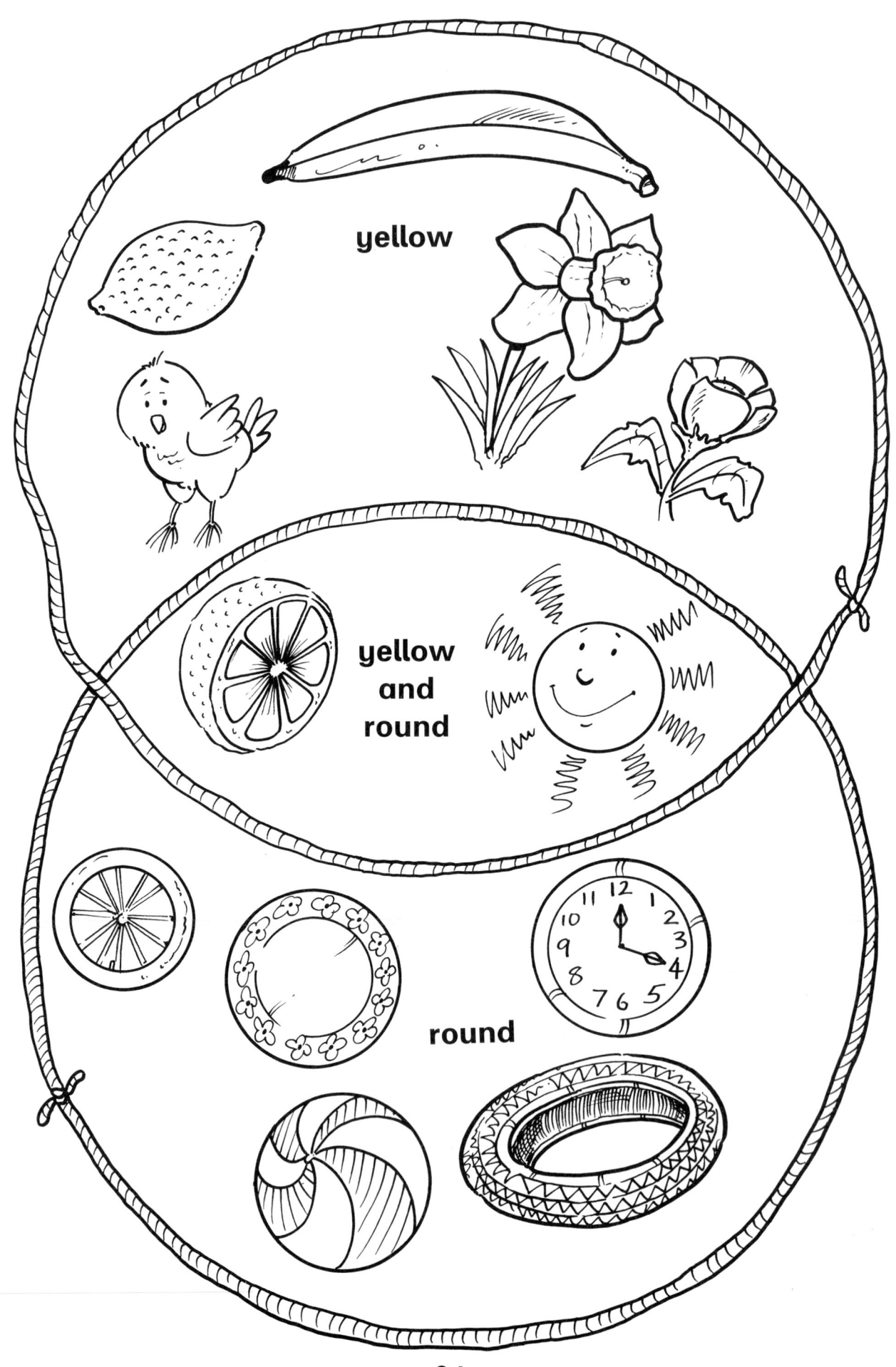

Story Board 8

Poor Jenny

| beginning | middle | end |

Zip's football

| beginning | middle | end |

Wishing

> I wish I may,
> I wish I might,
> Have the wish
> I wish tonight.

If you could make a wish, what would you wish for?

> I am the genie of the lamp. What is your wish?

Choices 10

Which three gifts would you choose?
Why?

Take it in turns to tell each other
what you have chosen and
why you chose them.

Question and Answer 11

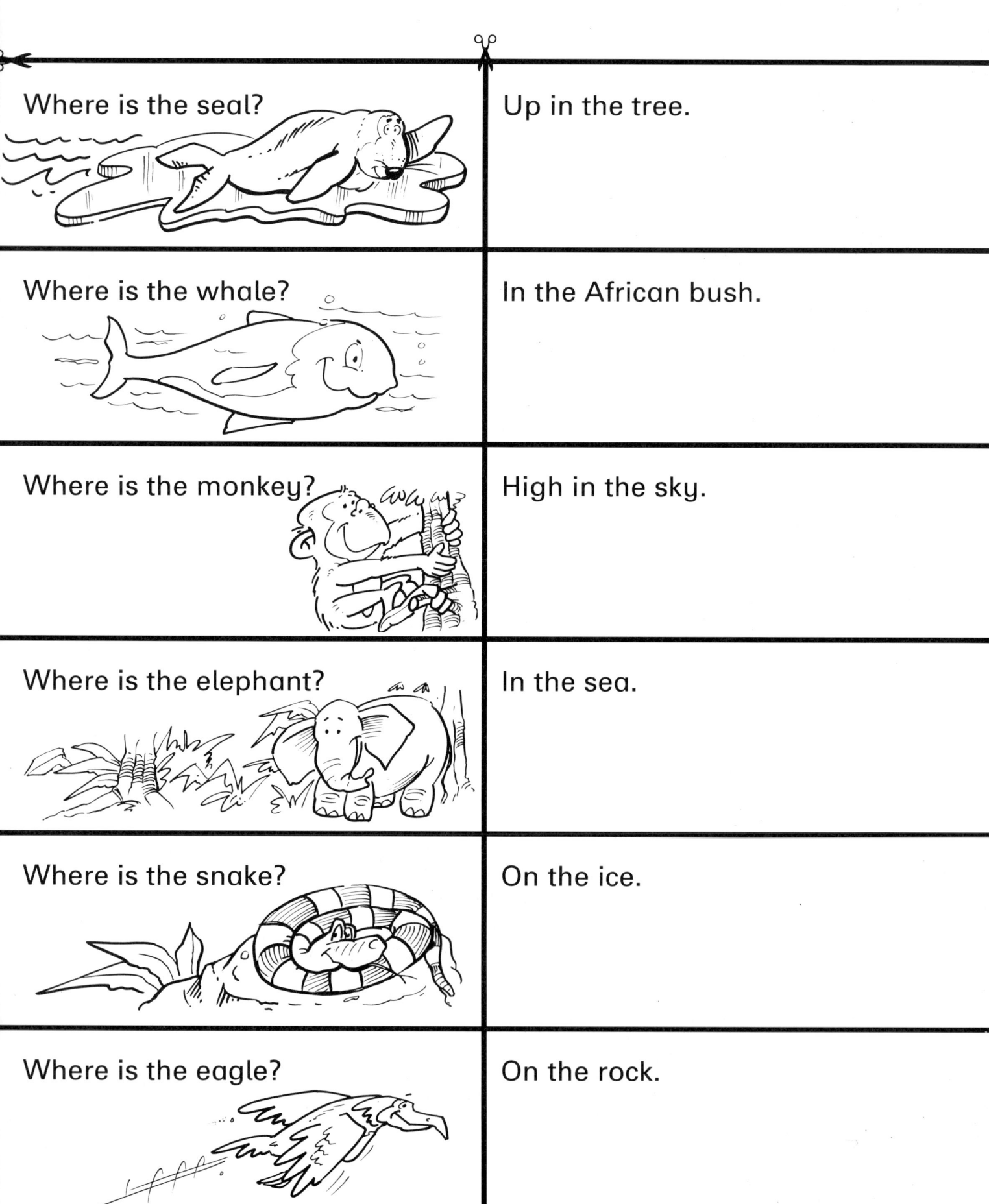

Where is the seal?	Up in the tree.
Where is the whale?	In the African bush.
Where is the monkey?	High in the sky.
Where is the elephant?	In the sea.
Where is the snake?	On the ice.
Where is the eagle?	On the rock.

My Giant Sandwich

What would you like in your sandwich?

I Didn't Mean To... 13

32

Caged   14

Sometimes tigers are kept like this.

This is how they like to be – free.

Would you like to be shut in a cage?
How would you feel?

happy   sad   pleased   cross   angry

Is it right to keep an animal in a cage?

Word Wall Puzzle 15

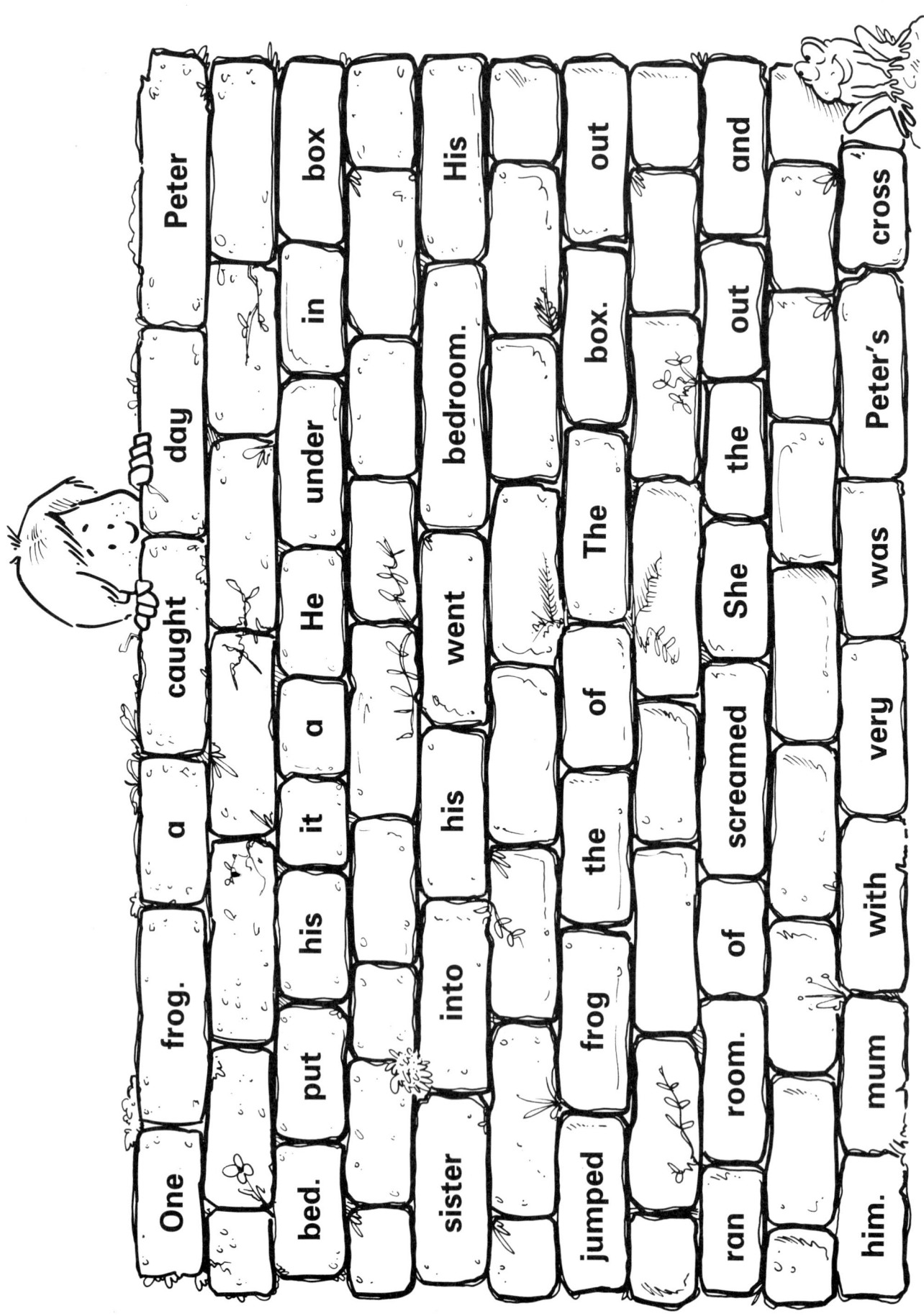

One day Peter caught a frog. He put it in a box under his bed. His sister went into his bedroom. The frog jumped out of the box. She screamed and ran out of the room. Peter's mum was very cross with him.

Party Time

16

When? _____

drink	food	games	friends

Make an invitation card for the party.

The Wind and the Sun   17

Who will make this man take off his coat –

the wind   or   the sun?

How will they do it?

Make up a play about what happens and what the wind and the sun say to each other.

My Home 18

Draw a picture of your home.
Put in it all the things you care about.
Tell your partner why you care about them.

> Talk about
>   why some things are the same and
>   why some things are different.

Favourite Things

19

Write your favourite things on the chart.
Talk about why you like them with your partner.

Name	Favourite colour	Favourite food	Favourite toy

Ask other children about their favourite things.
Now write them on your chart.

Goldilocks and the Three Bears 20

Your group needs
- 1 paper plate each for the face
- odd bits of wool and material
- glue
- felt pens
- an old ruler or card to make a handle.

Tell the story with your puppets.
Show your puppet play to your class.

Finding Out   21

Select objects and find out if they float or sink.

Fill in this chart to show what you have found out.

object	guess		result	
	float	sink	float	sink

40

Mystery Parcel 22

Who is the parcel for?
What is inside it?

Take it in turns to tell the group what you would like to find inside.
How many uses can your group think of for this box?

Spot the Changes 23

Talk about the two pictures with your partner.

Draw a ring round the things that are different in the second picture.

What am I Looking At? 24

Make a collection of objects for your tray.

Choose a thinker.

Guess what object is in the thinker's mind.

The one who guesses the object is the next thinker.

Guess What!

25

Choose one object.
Say five things about it.
Talk about things like

its shape

its size

what it is made of

where it can be found

who uses it.

44

Telephone Talk 1

26

Talk about the reasons why we use a telephone.
Choose one reason and make up a telephone call.
Perform it to your group.

Poems We Like 27

Choose a poem you like.
Read it to your friend.
Listen to your friend's poem.
Talk about why you chose your poems.

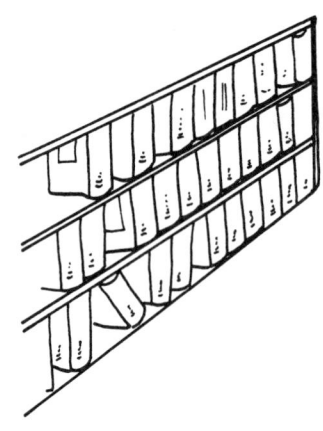

One way to learn a poem

Say it aloud over and over again.

Ask your friend to listen to you say it from memory.

If you get stuck ask your friend to tell you the next word.

Say it every day until you are sure of it.

Now begin to learn a new poem.

Toy Shop

28

Look at all the different kinds of toys.

Make a list of all the toys you can remember.
If you are REALLY stuck you may have one more QUICK look.

Our Senses 29

Talk about what you can see in the picture.

What would you
see
hear
touch
taste and
smell
if you were this child?

Our Senses – Likes and Dislikes 30

Things we like

see

hear

smell

taste

touch

Talk about things you like to **see**. Choose words that tell why you like to **see** them. Write them in the see column.
Do the same for **hear**, **smell**, **taste**, **touch**.

Now do the same for things you do not like.

Things we do not like

see

hear

smell

taste

touch

Calamity Kitchen

31

Talk about what is happening in the kitchen.

Is it a safe kitchen?

Could anything else happen?

50

Choosing Colours 32

Choose the colours you would like for these things and write them on the web.

Talk about your colours with your group.

Colours – Warm or Cool 33

Make a chart of warm colours and cool colours.

Colour chart

warm	cool
red	blue

Make a fold down the middle of a large sheet of paper.

Puddle warm colours on it.

Fold the paper and smooth it out.

Open it up and see what has happened.

Do the same with cool colours.

52

Colours for Reasons 34

Talk about the colours of these things.
Colour them in.

What colour is used on these signs. Why?

Sorting and Setting 2 | 35

Cut out these pictures.

Sort them into sets to show what they are made from.

Stick the sets on a large sheet of paper.

Can you sort them in a different way?

Cut up another sheet to make new sets.

Birthday Wheel 36

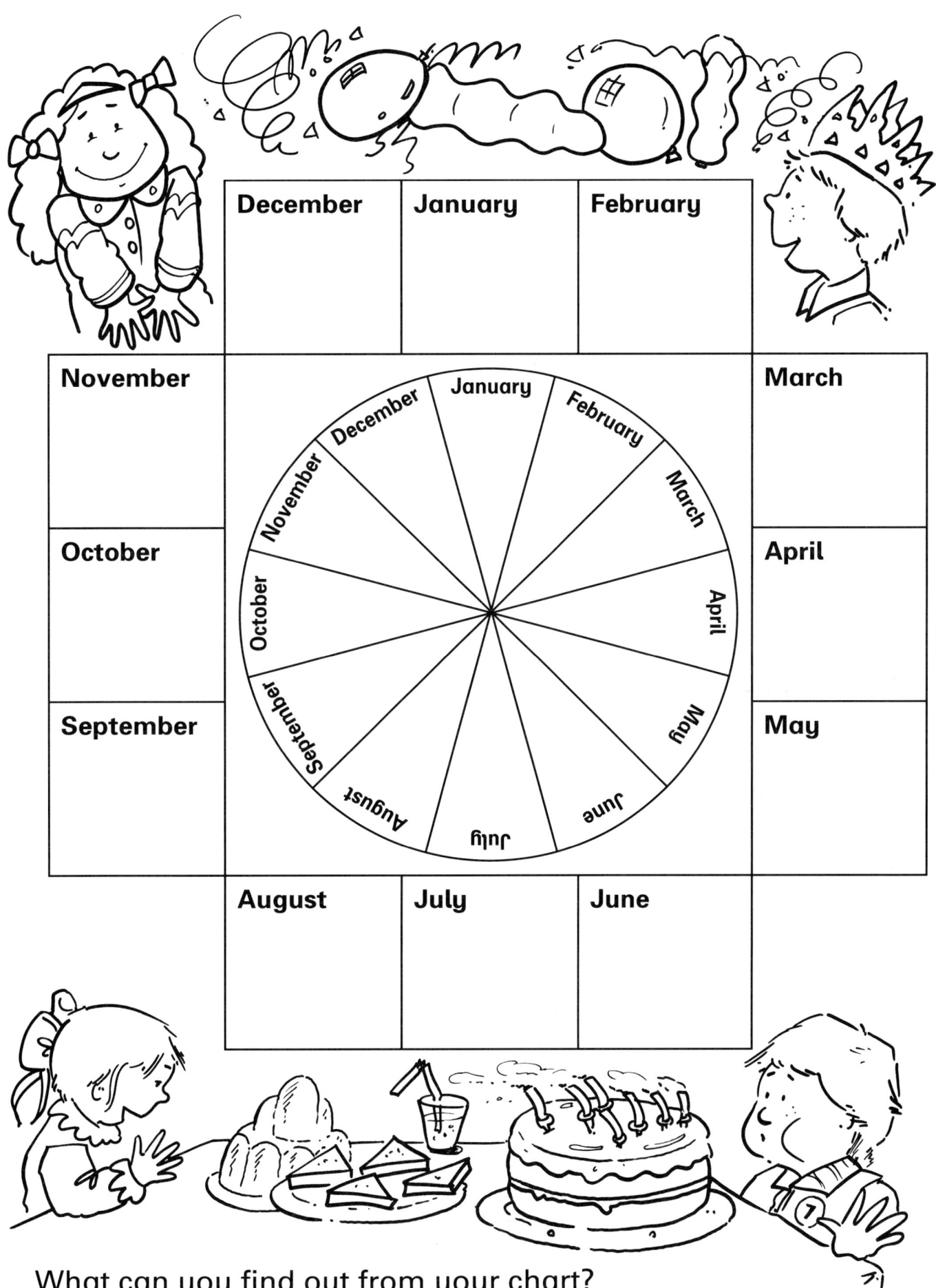

What can you find out from your chart?

Work 37

Talk about the work these people are doing.

What are the good and bad things about each job?

What work would you like to do? Why?

Sound Words 38

Make a chart of sounds you can make with your mouth, your hands or your feet.

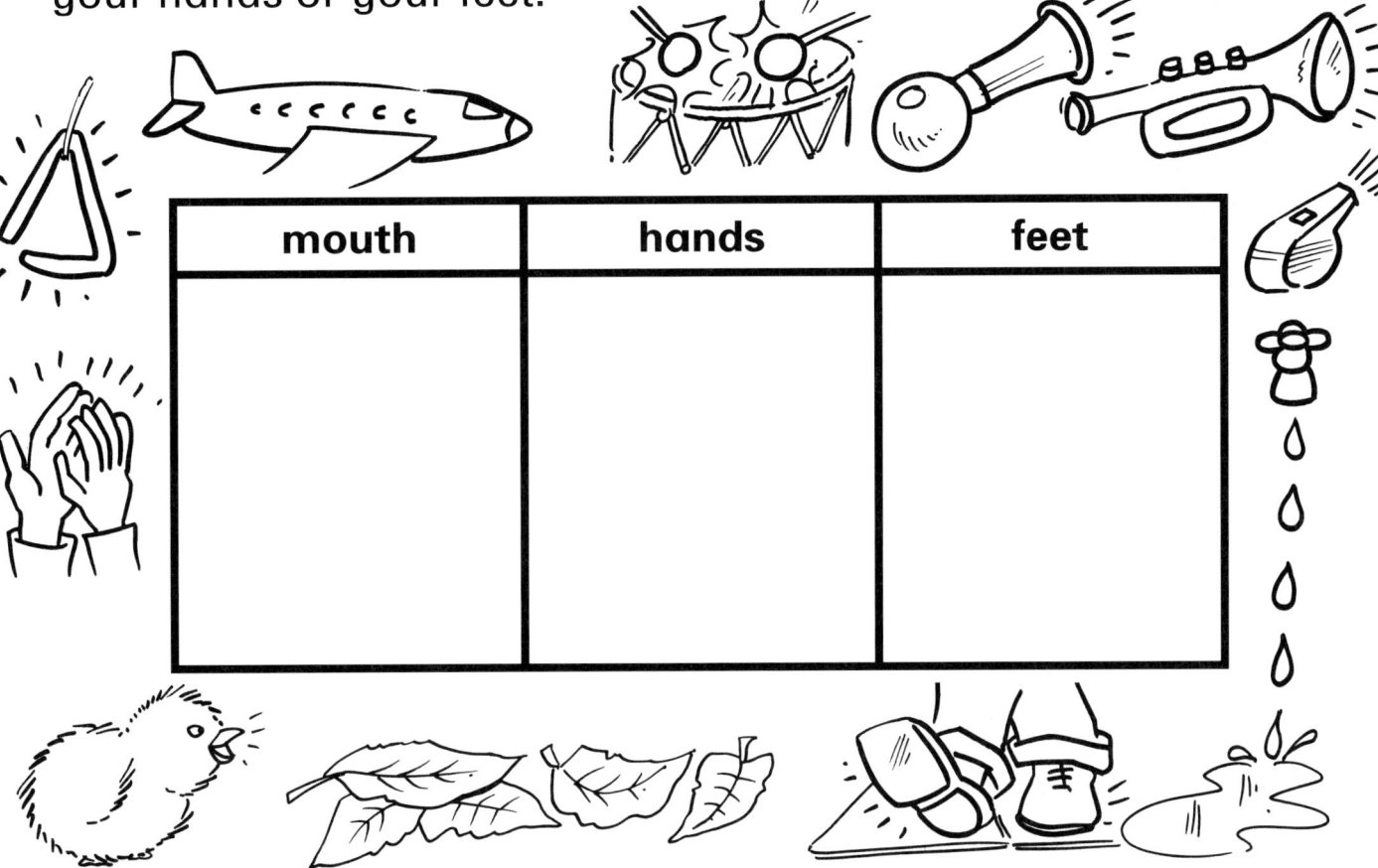

mouth	hands	feet

Make a book of sound words.
Use a different page for each kind of sound.

happy sounds — laughing
nasty sounds — shouting
music sounds — tinkle
people sounds — shuffle
sad sounds — sighing
weather sounds — pitter-patter
animal sounds — squeak, roar
house sounds — ring
traffic sounds — screech, roar
school sounds — bell

57

Telephone Talk 2

Choose one of these scenes and make up a telephone conversation with your partner.
Both try to change the other person's mind.

The wolf wants the little pig to go to market with him.

The Queen wants to visit Snow White with a magic apple.

The Giant wants Jack to return the magic harp.

Big Billy Goat Gruff wants the Troll to let them cross over the bridge.

The frog wants to come to the palace and have supper with the princess.

The child wants the giant to let them play in his garden.

Try another scene. Work on the one you like best so you can perform it to the class.

What's it all About? 40

What is happening in the picture?
What is the matter with the little girl?

Why is she feeling like that?
How could you help her?

What have you decided?
Choose one person to tell the class what your group thinks.

Owning Up   41

Talk about these stories and the endings.

Which ending would you choose? Why?

Is it easy to do the right thing?

What do you know? 42

You have just arrived by train.

Talk about this new place.
Ask yourselves these questions about everything.
  What is it?
  What does it tell you about this place?
  What happens there?

Would you like to live in this place?
Why?
Why not?

Teacher's Assessment Sheet

Record of the *First Speaking and Listening Kit* copymaster sheets completed and the National Curriculum statements they cover. Cross through sheet number as a record of the work the child has completed.

Child's name _____ **d.o.b.** _____ **Comments**

Level 1

a) Participate as speakers and listeners in group activities, including imaginative play — with help
1, 2, 4, 8, 9, 10, 12

b) Listen attentively, and respond, to stories and poems — with adult
13

c) Respond appropriately to simple instructions given by a teacher — with help
3, 6, 7, 11

Level 2

a) Participate as speakers and listeners in a group engaged in a given task
1, 2, 3, 4, 5, 6, 7, 9, 10, 11, 12, 13, 14, 15, 16, 17, 18, 19, 20, 21, 22

b) Describe an event, real or imagined, to the teacher or another pupil
9, 13, 18

c) Listen attentively to stories and poems, and talk about them
8, 13, 17, 20

d) Talk with the teacher, listen, and ask and answer questions
1, 2, 3, 9, 10, 13, 14, 19, 21, 23, 24

e) Respond appropriately to a range of more complex instructions given by a teacher, and give simple instructions
3, 6, 11, 15

Level 3

a) Relate real or imaginary events in a connected narrative which conveys meaning to a group of pupils, the teacher or another known adult
13, 20, 23, 25, 26, 27, 30, 31

b) Convey accurately a simple message
26, 39

c) Listen with an increased span of concentration to other children and adults, asking and responding to questions and commenting on what has been said
14, 23, 24, 25, 28, 29, 30, 31, 35, 36, 37, 40, 41, 42

d) Give, and receive and follow accurately, precise instruction when pursuing a task individually or as a member of a group
13, 15, 18, 19, 29, 31, 32, 33, 34, 36, 39

English writing — 8, 13, 16, 19

Maths sorting and setting — 7, 35, 36
graphs — 16, 19

Science living things — 6, 11
floating and sinking — 21
senses — 29, 30